The Ti

BY SUSAN HOLLIDAY

LDA

The Time Street Gang

The Time Street Gang
LL00756B
ISBN 1 85503 190 6

First published 1993
Reprinted 1994, 1996, 1999

Printed in the UK for LDA
LDA, Duke Street, Wisbech, Cambs, PE13 2AE, UK
2400 Turner Ave. NW, Grand Rapids, MI 49544, USA

1

Tom's Secret

'Please tell us,' said Dan.

'Just you wait!' said Tom. 'My dad sent it for my birthday! All the way from America. It has only just come!'

'It's nearer our birthday than yours,' said Em. 'You were ten *days* ago,' She held up her puppet. 'The same day as Jot.'

'That puppet's too old to keep!' said Dan.

Dan and Em were twins. They lived with their mum in Time Street, next door to Tom. After school they often met secretly in Tom's bedroom. The Time Street Gang was Dan's idea. How about going to another time he said one day.?

It was easy to keep secrets in Tom's house. His mum could not see very well and his dad was never there.

Dan looked round. 'Where is your secret?' he asked.

'In the attic,' said Tom.

The children stood up and said the Attic Password. Dan had made up the password for the Gang. One day he wrote down TOM, DAN, EM, then TOMDANEM, all together, like that. Then he changed the letters round to spell ' Demon Mat'.

'DEMON MAT DEMON MAT DEMON MAT,' said the Time Street Gang all together.

Tom picked up a torch and opened the little door by his bed. It led into the attic. It was very dark. They crept into the attic and Tom shut the door. Now there was no light at all. They all sat on an old mat and said the password again.

'DEMON MAT DEMON MAT DEMON MAT.'

Then Tom turned on his torch. He shone it round the attic.

There was the Time-machine they were making. There were the secret things they would take with them when they were ready. Dr Who – the mouse in a cage, the bundle of old clothes, the big black pan, the tinned food, the tin opener and the plastic bag full of grain. They had bought them all from the jumble sale at school.

Tom shone his torch on a box in the

corner of the attic. 'There it is!'

He picked up the box and brought it over to the mat. It was very light. He lifted up the lid. Inside the box was another box and inside that box was another box. Then another and another. The last box was lined with soft, light cotton wool. Tom felt inside the cotton wool. It was still there! The biggest egg he had ever seen.

'The biggest in the world,' he said proudly. 'My dad said so, that's why he sent it to me. He found it in the desert ...'

He turned off the torch and said very softly, 'This egg is millions of years old. It's a dinosaur's egg. That's what my dad said. A dinosaur's egg. We'll keep it here with the other secrets.'

At that moment there was a loud knock on the bedroom door. 'All out,' said Tom softly.

They crept out of the attic and Tom shut the little door. They all sat on Tom's bed as he said 'Come in then.'

It was Ben, the twins' half-brother, and his dog Jim. Ben was 16. He worked at the pet shop. He wrote poems about the pets and put them on the walls of the pet shop. He wanted to be a poet like his dad, who had gone back to Africa.

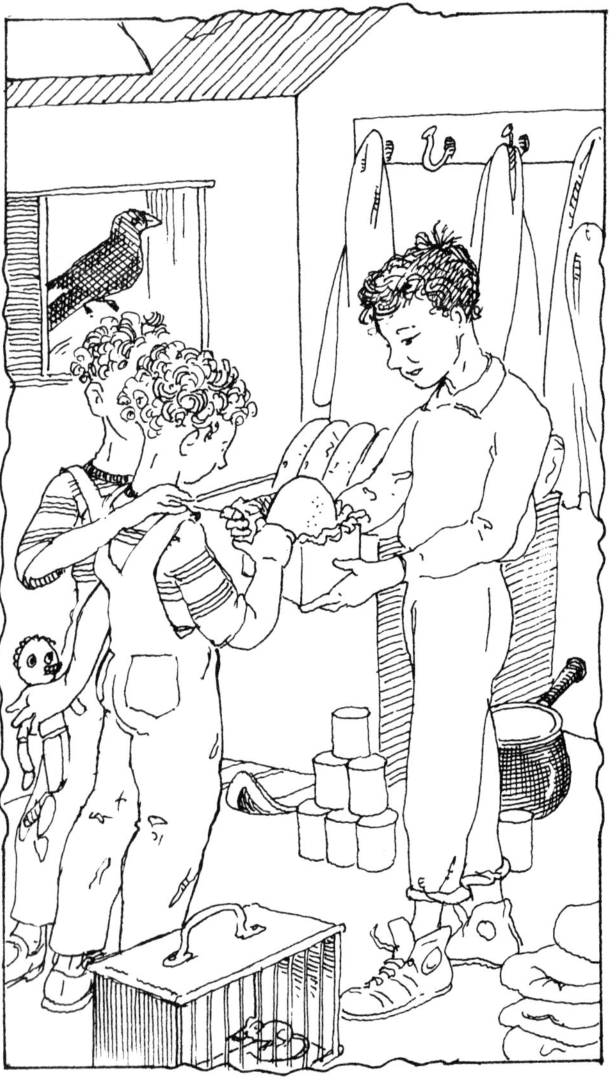

'Sit!' he said to Jim. Jim always did as he was told. He had been a guide dog for the blind. Ben loved animals. He had given Dr Who to Tom and the twins. But they never told Ben about the Time Street Gang. That was their secret.

'Tea's ready,' Ben said to the twins. 'My turn tonight as Mum's working.'

Ben picked up the twins, one under each arm, then put them down again. He was big and strong and they were small for their age. He went downstairs and Jim went after them. Tom's mum was in the hall. She stroked Jim and smiled.

'Thanks for having us, Mrs Ryan,' said the twins together. 'See you tomorrow.'

'They're no trouble,' said Mrs Ryan to Ben, 'Quiet as mice up there. All of them!'

She opened the door and Ben took the twins down the steps. Jim went after them. Then Mrs Ryan patted Tom on his dark head. He was nearly as big as she was.

'I've something to tell you,' she said, in a soft voice.

2

Aunt Pat

Mum made Tom a mug of tea.

'It's my eyes, Tom. I have to go to hospital tomorrow.'

'What for?'

'An operation. Aunt Pat will come to look after you.'

Tom put down his mug. 'I'll be all right, Mum. I'm 10 now.'

Mum smiled. 'That's not old enough to be left alone. Aunt Pat's all right. She lives alone but she will do her best.'

'I don't like her best,' said Tom. 'She's so tidy, and she's cross all the time!'

Not like Mum, he thought. Mum smiles. Mum understands. Mum liked him as he was. 'Dreamer,' she would say, 'just like your dad.' But she let him get on with his plans. She liked Dan and Em to help him make the Time-machine. Of course, she did not know it was a Time-machine. She only knew they were happy in the attic.

If only he could make an Eye-machine! He drank up his tea. Or a Bring-back-Dad-machine.

'How long will you be at the hospital?' he asked.

'Only a few days.'

'A few days is a long time with Aunt Pat!'

✧

The first day Mum was away Tom and the twins walked very slowly home from school.

'There's a skip,' said Tom to Dan. 'Let's have a look.'

He was taller than the twins. He looked in the yellow skip. There were some old pieces of wood, an old door, a roll of string, a bag of curlers and on top …

'A driving wheel,' he said. 'Just what we need to drive the Time-machine.'

He took it out and looked in the skip again.

They picked up more things and walked very slowly home.

Aunt Pat stood at the front door. Her arms were folded.

'Late!' she said. 'And who are you two?'

'Dan and Em,' said the twins together.

'And this is Jot,' said Em.

'Jot indeed! And what's all that?'

'To make things,' said Tom.

'You can put that back where you found it,' said Aunt Pat. 'You may fool your mother but you can't fool me.'

'I'll put it away,' said Tom.

Aunt Pat frowned. 'Put it back where you found it. Then come straight home, Tom. Alone. It's all I can do to look after *you*!'

She shut the door and looked at them through the kitchen window. She began to peel potatoes.

'We have a ladder,' said Dan to Tom. 'While she's in the kitchen we can go into our house, put the ladder over the fence and climb up to your bedroom.'

'I'll keep her in the kitchen,' said Em. Tom and Dan ran off. Em put Jot against the kitchen window. She made her dance up and down. Aunt Pat looked grumpy and came to the front door.

'Why don't you go home?'

'I want to cheer you up,' said Em. 'Meet Jot. I want to do a puppet show on the window while you peel potatoes. Peeling potatoes is so boring.'

'You can say that again,' said Aunt Pat sharply.

There was a noise at the back of the house.

'What's that?'

'Our dog Jim,' said Em. 'He sometimes jumps the fence.'

'Dogs!' said Aunt Pat. 'I hate dogs!'

She turned her back. 'I must go and see. Dogs indeed!'

3

Em Pretends!

Em let out a loud scream and Aunt Pat turned round.

'My ankle!' yelled Em. 'My ankle!'

'What about your ankle?'

Em was lying at the bottom of the steps. Jot lay beside her.

'It hurts! It hurts! I fell down the steps. OH! OH! OH! Can you get someone, Aunt Pat?'

Her screams grew louder and louder.

Aunt Pat stood still, then she ran down the steps.

'Get up, Em!'

'I can't! I can't!'

Aunt Pat looked up and down the road. 'Tom is a big boy. He will lift you when he comes back.'

'He's at the dump. It's ten minutes from here. OH! OH! OH! Aunt Pat, can't you get him?'

Aunt Pat frowned. She looked up and down the road but there was no one else in sight. Em began to scream again.

'Now stop that screaming,' said Aunt Pat. 'If I must go, at least stop that screaming!' She frowned again.

She took off her apron, folded it and gave it to Em. 'Look after this.'

When Aunt Pat was round the corner Em stood up. She ran through the house and called up to Tom. He was at the top of the ladder.

'She heard you,' said Em, 'so I fell down the steps. She's gone to look for you at the dump!'

Dan was half-way up the ladder with the steering wheel.

'The last thing,' he cried.

Em ran back through the house and sat on the pavement again. She played with Jot until she heard Aunt Pat's footsteps.

'OH! OH! OH! she screamed again.

'Shut up!' said Aunt Pat. 'I've had enough. Tom is nowhere to be seen.'

At that moment Tom and Dan ran along the pavement.

'What is it, Em?' they said together.

'My ankle!'

'Where have *you* been?' asked Aunt

Pat.

'To the skip,' said Tom.

Aunt Pat turned to Em. 'I thought you said they were at the rubbish dump.'

'That's what I call a skip,' said Em. 'It has rubbish inside.'

'And where's my apron?'

It had blown down the street.

'It was the wind,' said Em. 'I couldn't go after it.'

'Children!' said Aunt Pat. 'Thank goodness I never had any children. Now!'

She turned to Tom and Dan. 'Carry her next door. Go on! Carry her.'

Tom and Dan made a seat of their hands and carried Em slowly next door. Mum was not in yet, nor was Ben. They sat on the kitchen floor and laughed and laughed.

'That will show her,' said Tom.

'You won't want to stay with her,' said Em.

'Now we have the driving wheel we can soon take off,' said Dan.

He looked in the fridge. There was nothing but eggs.

'Mum never shops,' he said. 'Just because she doesn't like eating ...'

'Here you are,' said Tom. He had a

packet of sweets in his pocket. 'My mum loves eating. She says I'm a growing lad.'

Dan looked up at Tom. 'Some of us have brains instead!' he said.

4

A Smell of Burning

After tea Aunt Pat put on the TV. She said, 'It's to take my mind off children!'

Tom went up to the attic. The Time-machine would take his mind off Mum.

They had put a wooden box on Dad's old skis. In the box were three old car seats to sit on. Beside the box was an old computer Ben had been given. Tom said the computer might take them through time. You never know, he said, it might work.

Ben let Dan have the computer. Dan liked to make things work. For a long time Dan tried to make the computer work. At last he understood it. Now he was trying to find the 'time' programme. He said he would find it before long.

Tom looked at his dinosaur egg. It would be nice to go back to the time of the dinosaurs, to know what it was really like.

He tied the driving wheel to two sticks he had found in the back garden. He made holes in the box and tied the sticks to them with the curlers and string they had found in the skip. Then he sat on a car seat in the box.

If only Mum could come with them! It would take her mind off her sight. If only she could go back to the time of the dinosaurs with them.

'Bang! Bang!'

Tom jumped up and ran out of the attic. He opened his bedroom door. There was Aunt Pat standing with her arms folded. She frowned.

'Don't you lock this door on me,' she said. 'What if there's a fire and you couldn't find the key?'

'There never has been a fire,' said Tom.

'You never know,' said Aunt Pat. She looked round his bedroom. 'This room is a mess. I have never seen such a mess in my life. I'll have to clean it.'

'I'll clean it,' said Tom. 'I'll clean it tomorrow.'

'And what's in there?' said Aunt Pat.

Tom had left the attic door open! He didn't know what to say.

'A...a...a...a thing that puts out a fire.'

'What do you mean, a thing that puts out fire? Show me.'

Tom was in luck! Just at that moment, when he did not know what to do, a smell of burned sausages came up the stairs. Aunt Pat turned and ran down. Tom sat down on the bed. He could not believe his luck!

'That's what comes from trying to please you!' said Aunt Pat as Tom came down for tea.

The phone rang and Aunt Pat ran into the hall.

'Yes, yes, yes,' she said. Then she made a long speech about children. She put down the phone and went back into the kitchen.

Tom stood up. 'How's Mum?'

'That was not your mother,' said Aunt Pat. 'That was Sister Bright, a friend of mine from the hospital.'

'What did she say?'

'She says your mother's all right.'

'When can I see her?' said Tom.

'Tomorrow after school.'

'Not before?'

'No!' Aunt Pat frowned. 'And don't be late. And while we're at it, I don't want to see those friends of yours again. Not ever. One child is quite enough for me!'

✧

'She has a bandage over her eyes,' Tom told Dan after his visit to Mum.

Dan nodded.

'But she's cheerful. You know my mum.'

'Your mum's one of the best,' said Dan.

'She makes it nice in your house,' said Em.

'It's a no-go house now.'

'What do you mean?'

'Aunt Pat. She says one child's enough.'

'Sounds like my mum.'

'What about Dr Who? We don't want Aunt Pat getting at our mouse.'

'Or my dinosaur egg,' said Tom.

'Or the tinned food,' said Em. 'She won't go into the attic, will she?'

'Not if I can help it!' said Tom.

5

Gone!

When Tom went into his bedroom he knew that she had been there. Everything looked different. His bed, his table, his books, the windows, the pictures – they all looked different, as if someone had cleaned them hard.

He looked under his pillow. His torch was still there. He knelt down and went into the attic. He shone his torch into the dark.

He could not believe his eyes. He shut them and opened them to make sure.

There was nothing there.

Dr Who, the dinosaur egg, the tinned food, the Time-machine, all had gone. In their place was a clean black hole and the smell of bleach.

Tom shut his eyes again. It could not be true! But it was. However hard he looked, the attic was empty. It was as if the Time-machine had been only a dream.

'Dad, Dad,' he cried. 'If you'd been here this wouldn't have happened. Where's my dinosaur egg? Where's she put my dinosaur egg?'

He began to touch the wooden walls and the floor as if he were half-blind, like Mum. But there was nothing there. Nothing at all. He crept out of the attic and shut the door.

For a while he sat in his bedroom. He was very angry. What could he do? After a while he ran downstairs and into the kitchen. Aunt Pat was sitting at the table, reading a book. She did not look up.

'I need a rest,' she said, 'after all that work!'

Tom stood in front of her.

'What have you done with my things? What have you done with them?'

'You mean that rubbish?'

'I hate you,' said Tom. He ran outside.

Aunt Pat ran after him.

'Manners!' she called, 'that's what's wrong with you lot. No manners! If your mum could see she would have had a fit.'

'Don't you talk about my mum,' said Tom.

'Come back,' said Aunt Pat. 'I've done salad and tuna fish.'

'I hate salad and tuna fish,' said Tom. He was so angry he turned his back on Aunt Pat and ran next door.

Ben opened the door. Inside the house there was a smell of fried eggs.

'Come for tea?'

To his shame Tom began to cry. He sniffed and blew his nose.

'Hey! Come in. It can't be as bad as that.'

'Will you take me to see Mum, Ben? I want to tell her what's happened.'

Ben sat Tom down at the table and gave him some chips. Em and Dan were eating their tea. They looked up.

'You said your mum was all right,' said Dan.

Tom wiped his eyes and picked up a chip. As he thought of Mum he felt better.

'She *is* all right. It's Aunt Pat!' 'She's taken everything.'

'What do you mean?'

'Dr Who, the dinosaur's egg, the Time-machine, everything. It's all gone.'

'Where's it gone?' said Dan.

Tom shook his head. 'I don't know.'

'Everything?' said Em over her mug of tea.

'Everything. Nothing's left.'

Tom looked up at Ben, then back at Em and Dan.

'I didn't mean to tell Ben! For a moment I forgot! I forgot the Time Street Gang is a secret.'

'We all forgot,' said Dan. He looked at Ben.

'We have this secret gang.'

'The Time Street Gang,' said Em.

'Will you be in it?' said Tom. 'We need your help.'

'What do you do?' said Ben.

'We meet in the attic. We have a password. We have secret plans. We were making a Time-machine. We were going back to the time of the dinosaurs. That was before Aunt Pat came. Now she has taken everything. There is nothing left. What can we do?'

Ben gave Tom a mug of tea. 'Here, drink this. It will make you feel better. I would love to be in the Time Street Gang. And there is always something we can do.'

6

At Midnight

Ben shut his eyes and thought. The children drank their tea.

'I know what we can do.'

The Time Street Gang looked at him.

'We'll get them back. That's what we'll do.'

Tom stood up. 'How?'

'You must go back and find out what Aunt Pat's done with them. Now.'

'The witch! She won't tell me.'

'You mustn't be rude, Tom. You must ask her politely. It's the only way. Then come back to tell us after tea.'

'I want egg and chips,' said Tom, 'not tuna fish and salad.'

'You can have tea with us tomorrow.'

✧

Aunt Pat was in the kitchen. She was

watching TV.

'I'm sorry,' said Tom.

Aunt Pat folded her arms and frowned. She still looked at the TV.

'And well you might be. You have much to learn, my boy. Your mother was always soft!'

'May I have my tea?'

Aunt Pat sniffed. 'It's there for you, isn't it?'

Tom sat down at the table. It was hard to eat the tuna fish and salad.

'It's lovely,' he said, gulping.

'Of course it's lovely,' said Aunt Pat to the TV. 'I know all about food, I do.'

Tom wanted to say, 'So does Mum,' but he stopped himself. He thought of the fried eggs and chips and he wanted to say, 'So does Ben.'

Instead he gulped and said, 'The house is lovely and clean.'

At last Aunt Pat turned to look at him.

'I do my best,' she said, 'I always do my best.'

Tom nodded.

'It must have been hard to get rid of all that rubbish.'

'Hard? Of course it was hard. All the way to that bonfire on the heath. Of

course I do it every year. Only I take my garden things. Leaves and sticks and things like that. Not the sort of rubbish you keep in the attic!'

Tom nodded. 'Everybody takes things to the bonfire.'

He felt sick.

'May I get down?'

'Of course.'

'Thank you, Aunt Pat. May I go next door? I need a book for homework.'

Aunt Pat looked at her watch. 'Five minutes. Mind you're back in five minutes.'

Tom ran next door.

'I've got five minutes,' he told Ben. 'The things are on the bonfire. It's Guy Fawkes Night on Saturday ...'

'Our birthday,' said Em.

'By Saturday it will all be gone.'

'We'll go up there tonight,' said Ben. At midnight. Can you get away?'

'Of course I can,' said Tom. 'Aunt Pat always sleeps well. She says she's very tired. She snores.'

Ben laughed. 'Have you got a clock?'

Tom pointed to his watch. 'Dad gave it to me. It's American. It has an alarm.'

'Be here at midnight,' said Ben as Tom ran down the steps.

That night Tom set his watch but he woke before the alarm went off. It was nearly midnight. He crept to the window. It was dark and the stars were shining. He hoped Dr Who was still in his cage. He hoped his mouse was not too cold. It looked very cold outside. And his dinosaur egg – was it broken?

He listened to Aunt Pat. First she snored, then her bed creaked.

'I hope she's still asleep,' he thought.

He put on his clothes and took a blanket in case they found Dr Who. He opened his bedroom door and crept down the stairs. Then he stopped. Below him he heard another door open and there was Aunt Pat! She stood on the stairs. She pulled at a curler in her hair.

'Not like they used to make them!'

She pulled her dressing-gown round her. 'What a cold house. I'll be glad to get home. As for Tom ...'

Tom watched her go down to the loo. He pulled the blanket over his head in case she turned round.

He looked through a little opening in the blanket. On the bottom stair Aunt Pat stopped and stood still. She pulled at another curler and began to say things. This time Tom could not hear. He pulled the blanket back so he could see what Aunt Pat was doing. She must have heard him!

She turned round as if she knew he was there!

7

On the Bonfire

Aunt Pat screamed.

'A burglar! Help! Help!'

Tom ran back to his bedroom. He opened the window and jumped into bed. He pulled the bed-clothes up and shut his eyes just as Aunt Pat came in.

She ran to the window and looked out. She heard a door squeak. The burglar must be next door! She turned back to Tom, who still had his eyes shut.

'Sleeping when there's a burglar!' said Aunt Pat sharply.

She shut the window. 'Well, I'm not going next door!'

She passed Tom's bed. 'At least *he* can't get into trouble while he's asleep.'

Tom kept his eyes shut. Did Aunt Pat always talk to herself? People on their own often did! At last she went out. He waited for her to close the bedroom door, then he crept out again.

'It's all right,' said Ben, 'we saw her at the window so we hid.'

They ran down the road. It led to another road that led to the heath. The night was cold and clear. There was a slight frost. Ben had a torch and Tom and Dan and Em followed the small light.

At night the heath looked like another land. A land of long ago, thought Tom. He looked round for the bonfire. For a minute it looked like a giant animal under the huge sky.

They went round the bonfire. Dan shone his torch up and down.

'There it is!' said Em loudly.

'Shhh!' said Ben softly.

The Time-machine was under a pile of sticks and leaves.

'Careful,' said Tom as Ben tried to pull it out. The tinned food and the bag of clothes rolled out but the machine was broken. The computer was on its side as if someone had tried to pull it away. The driving wheel and the skis had come apart.

'All our work for nothing,' said Tom. He hoped the others would not see the tears in his eyes.

'I wonder where Dr Who is. And what

about my egg?'

Ben pulled at the bonfire.

'There's the cage,' said Em softly. Dr Who was not inside.

'What's that?' said Em.

It was a box but there was no dinosaur egg inside. 'The egg has gone,' said Tom.

He walked away from the others. What would Dad say when he knew the egg had gone?

'I'm not going home,' he told Ben. 'That old witch! I hate her!'

'You have to go back,' said Ben. 'Think of your mum. I have some food. Let's eat it and have a think.'

They sat a little way away and ate biscuits.

'It's like another world,' said Em.

Tom looked round. The moon shone overhead. At the edge of the heath the chimneys stood tall in the sky like small heads of dinosaurs. From here the bonfire also looked like a dinosaur. A dinosaur who was asleep.

'The moon's the same,' he said.

'Same as when?' said Dan.

'Same as the time of the dinosaurs.'

'I have an idea,' said Ben.

He stood up and went over to the

broken Time-machine. He moved it further away from the bonfire. He put back the computer and the driving wheel. He pushed down the car seats.

'We'll take off,' he said. 'Come on, sit in the machine. I'll drive!'

Dan and Em ran over to the machine. Tom went slowly. How could they go in a broken machine?

'It's like you said,' said Ben, 'everything looks old tonight. We'll travel right back. Get in, you lot.'

At last Tom felt excited. The air was cool, the moon was bright. They were the only people who were awake.

Ben sat in front. He told the children to close their eyes.

'We're going to travel a long, long way,' he said. 'Keep your eyes shut! Hold on tight!'

8

The Journey

Tom shut his eyes. The air was cool. The moonlight shone through his eyelids. Ben made a low hum that grew louder and louder. The Time-machine was warming up.

'Keep your eyes shut and imagine or it won't work,' said Ben softly.

The hum was loud and steady. They were off!

Tom felt the cool air go past his face. The light of the moon grew in his eyes. He felt the sky winds go past. Time opened out like a dream. He kept his eyes shut. He wanted the time dream to go on. The Time-machine jolted as they make their way.

'It's the Ice Age,' said Ben softly. 'The moon is shining on the ice. Look out! The polar bears are coming.

'That was lucky! We missed a glacier. Up

we go now. Up and up.

'It's getting warmer now. The Ice Age is a long way off. It's cold up here but now the earth is hot.

'We're coming down again. There's a herd of elephants and monkeys. There's a herd of rhinos crossing the heath. There are people running about. There are more monkeys.

'Here we go – up and up again. Keep your eyes shut! Up and up and up. We're near the moon now. It's hard to breathe. Come on. Breathe in, breathe out, all of you. In out, in out.

'Now the Time-machine is taking us down. Down and down and down. Hold on, hold on tight!

'It's night and I can't see where we are going to land. I don't know the place but I can see the dinosaurs. Look out. Look out. Hold on!'

Ben's hum grew louder and there was a huge jolt.

Tom and Dan and Em rolled on to the grass. Tom opened his eyes and sat up.

There they were – the herd of black dinosaurs, and nearby a huge dinosaur sleeping with his head down. Above was the moon, just as it was in their time. There

was no noise at all.

'Get back into the machine,' said Ben after a while. 'We can't stay. We have a long way to go back.'

They climbed back into the Time-machine.

'Shut your eyes,' said Ben. The children shut their eyes.

Tom felt as if he was going through space, through time, as he did in his dreams.

'Now we're back in the Ice Age,' said Tom. 'It's getting colder. We're off again. Here's America. We must be coming back to our time. The sky-scrapers are tall – now we're over the desert.'

Tom saw his dad digging for eggs. He waved to him.

'Hi, Dad!' he said so no one else could hear. 'When I'm older I'll come and see you. We'll look for eggs together.'

'Hold on,' said Tom, 'we're coming down now.'

There was a huge jolt and the children were thrown out on to the grass. Tom lay there with his eyes shut. He did not want the adventure to stop.

'Come on,' said Ben, shaking him. 'We have to get back.'

'That was great,' said Tom.

He looked at the Time-machine. By now it was in pieces and Ben was throwing them on to the bonfire. But somehow it did not matter. Not now they had been for a ride.

'I'll keep the computer,' said Dan. 'You never know.'

Ben held it in his arms as they went back home.

'See you tomorrow,' Tom whispered as he climbed up the steps to his front door.

He crept inside. Aunt Pat was snoring loudly. He crept past her bedroom and into his own. He looked out of the window. The moon had moved over the houses.

Tom undressed. He fell asleep straight away. He dreamed he was riding on a dinosaur and Dad was behind him. He only woke because there was a loud bang at his door.

'I've never known anyone sleep like you,' shouted Aunt Pat. 'Get up, lazy bones. Your yoghurt is ready on the table. Get a move on!'

9

Birthday Treat

Dan and Em sat on the front steps. They did not dare come nearer. Aunt Pat was looking through the kitchen window.

'Look at this one,' said Em. Tom looked at the birthday card.

'The 10 today twins!' he read. The 1 was a thin girl and the 0 was a fat boy.

'From Ben,' said Em. 'He says Dan will soon be fat.'

'Why?' said Tom. Dan looked very thin to him.

'Always hungry,' said Em.

Now Tom gave the twins his card. He had made it this morning in bed. It was a picture of the Time-machine.

'Now you're 10 you'll go anywhere,' it said.

'Thanks,' said Em.

'We're going to McDonald's today,' said Dan, 'then on to the fireworks. For a birthday treat. It's good having our birthday on Guy Fawkes Night. Will you come with us, Tom?'

'You bet!' said Tom.

He looked up at Aunt Pat. He was always hungry now!

Dan said their mum was paying but she could not come. She had to work Saturdays.

✧

'But Ben's coming,' said Em, 'after work.'

Ben was late. He had been on the phone, he said. He had a big plastic bag.

'For left-overs,' he said. 'Jim loves left-overs! But you must have what you like.'

The children had nearly everything. Quarter-pounders, chicken nuggets, cheeseburgers, chips, coke to wash it down. They had lots of straws and paper napkins and paper cups.

As he ate Tom thought about the Time-machine. It would soon go up in flames. Just like that. And Dr Who and the egg? What had become of them?

Ben looked at his watch.

'It's nearly time for the fireworks. Come on, everyone! Eat up!'

The fireworks took Tom's mind off the Time-machine. The sky went red and yellow and blue and green and white. The rockets went up and up as if they were Time-machines. The bangers made him jump.

At last a man lit the bonfire. 'Keep right back,' he shouted.

Guy Fawkes was on top of the bonfire. He went red as he burned. His tall hat burned first, then his coat, then his trousers. Then he fell down. Tom remembered the time when Dad went with him to the fireworks. It was a very long time ago.

A man was selling hot dogs and Ben bought some more.

'I *will* get fat now,' said Dan.

'You'll never get fat,' said Tom.

At last the bonfire died down and people went away.

But Ben did not hurry them home. 'Let's have a look round,' he said.

The bonfire was still hot but the flames were now small. Everything had turned to ash, or almost everything.

'There's the driving wheel,' said Tom, pointing to a half-burned wheel.

'There's one of the seats,' said Dan.

But there was very little left. Tom felt sad.

There was nothing more to look forward to. It had been a dream, a good one. Nothing would be the same again!

'Stop crying,' said Em. 'We can make another Time-machine.'

Tom blew his nose loudly. 'Dad will never give me another egg,' he said.

'Don't cry,' said Ben. 'There's a really good surprise waiting for you.'

10

The Surprise

Dan and Em looked up at Tom's house.

'We'd better not come in.'

But Ben was jumping up the steps two at a time.

'Come on,' he said, swinging the doggy bag.

Tom heard Jim bark but it was not from next door. It was from his house, behind his door.

The door opened slowly. Tom couldn't believe his eyes. There was Jim wagging his tail and Mum smiling down at them.

Tom jumped up the steps and hugged Mum.

'Why didn't you tell me?'

'Surprise,' said Ben. 'Aunt Pat went for your mum then went off home. I left Jim to help. He is a great help!'

Ben put his hand in the doggy bag and threw Jim half a beefburger.

'I kept it for him,' said Ben.

Mum smiled. 'I can't tell you how lovely it is to be back.'

'It's all that counts,' thought Tom, 'having Mum back.'

Ben and the twins went inside too. Everyone spoke at once. It was like another party, only this time it was Tom's. He looked round.

'Has she really gone?' he said.

'Aunt Pat? She wouldn't even wait to say goodbye.'

'I don't care!' said Tom. 'I don't care if I never see her again.'

That night he was too excited to sleep. He went over to the window and looked at the moon. He began to count the stars but there were too many.

Then he heard a squeak. He turned round. Where did it come from? He picked up his torch and shone it round the room. There was no one there. He put out the torch and there it was again. A little squeak. It came from the attic.

Tom opened the attic door and put on his torch. There, sitting up in the light of his torch, was a mouse. It was white with white whiskers. It was Dr Who!

Tom smiled and spoke softly. 'I knew

you'd escape,' he said. 'I knew it, I knew it.'

Dr Who sat up as if he were begging.

Tom smiled. 'if only Aunt Pat could see you now!'

Mum and Dr Who in one go. He couldn't believe his luck! Things were looking up at last!

The next day Tom took Mum toast and tea in bed. Then Dan and Em called round.

'He's back!' said Tom.

'Who?' said the twins together.

'Dr Who. He's in the attic. Come and see.'

'Lovely to see you,' shouted Mrs Ryan as they ran upstairs past her bedroom.

'Glad you're back,' shouted the twins.

Tom shut his door and opened the attic door. He shone his torch inside.

'What a horrible smell,' said Em.

'Bleach,' said Tom.

Now there was no sign of Dr Who.

'They hide in the day,' said Dan. 'Don't worry! I'll get another cage off Ben. He has some old ones in the shop. If you put out some cheese Dr Who will come back. Then you can look after him. You'll see.'

They crept out of the attic and shut the

door.

'Ben bought us a video for our birthday,' said Em. 'You'll never guess what it's called.'

'Dr Who?'

'No!' Em couldn't wait. '*The Time Machine*. We're having it this afternoon. Do you want to come round?'

'You bet!' said Tom.

It was an old film from an old story by someone called H.G. Wells. It was like a film about their Time-machine. It was as if they were visiting all the places.

When it was over Dan stood up.

'We'll make another Time-machine,' he said. 'You'll see. This time we'll go to the future!'

'Doughnuts for tea,' said Ben. 'Mum left them. She's round at Roger's.'

'We think she's in love,' said Em.

'What's her boyfriend like?' said Tom.

Ben laughed. 'He bought the doughnuts and milk shakes! He's trying to keep in with us!'

'Not like Aunt Pat,' said Tom.

'Nothing is as bad as Aunt Pat,' said Em.

Then Ben said he would take them back to the bonfire. 'You never know what you might find. You never know!'

11

Where is Ben?

The next day the children met Ben at the pet shop. He picked up a plastic bag and took it with him.

'It's cold!' said Tom. What was the use of going back to the bonfire? There was nothing left. Nothing at all.

A wind blew across the heath. The bonfire was still smoking. Ash was everywhere. Ash and smoke. The smoke blew in the wind, first this way and then that. It was getting dark.

'There's nothing left at all,' said Tom sadly.

'Yes there is!' said Em. She pointed to an old box that was only half-burned.

Tom looked at the box. 'That isn't …' he began.

'Yes, it is,' said Em. 'The dinosaur box. That's what it is.'

Ben picked up a stick and pulled the

box off the bonfire.

'The inside's not burned,' said Tom, 'but there's nothing in it. Nothing at all.'

They all looked into the box.

'Maybe ...' said Ben, but he didn't stay to look. He went slowly round the bonfire, poking the ash with the stick.

'Hey!' he shouted. 'Come over here quickly.'

Tom and Dan and Em looked up.

'What's the matter?' asked Tom.

'You won't believe it,' shouted Ben. 'I hardly believe it myself. But it's here! It really is.'

'What's here?' shouted Tom.

The wind blew smoke into his eyes and he could not see Ben. Dan and Em looked for Ben too but the smoke was in their eyes as well.

By now it was dark. There was no sound on the heath except the wind blowing. What had happened? Where had Ben gone? Had he found the burned-out Time-machine and gone away?

'My eyes hurt,' said Em.

'I can't see anything any more,' said Dan. He rubbed his eyes with his sleeve.

'Nor can I,' said Tom.

The children stood still. There was no

sound except the wind.

'Ben's gone away,' said Tom at last. 'He's gone in the Time-machine. Perhaps he's already in the future!'

'Don't be daft,' said Dan. 'The computer's at home. He couldn't get away without the computer.'

'You don't know,' said Tom. But he did know and he wanted to cry.

It was getting darker. There were no stars. There was only the wind and the smoke and the cold that made their noses run.

'We should never have come,' said Em.

Then there was a crackling noise. They stood still, unable to move. Perhaps there was magic in the fire!

There was still no sign of Ben.

Em started to cry, so Dan took her hand.

'Don't be daft,' he said. 'We'll go slowly round the bonfire.'

'There might be magic in the fire,' said Tom as they walked round.

12

Ben's Find

They held hands and crept round the fire. The smoke blew this way and that. They could hardly see.

'Keep away!' said a voice softly. The children looked round but they could see no one.

'Who's there?' said Dan.

It was Ben! He was lying full length on the grass with his hands round something.

'Keep away!' he said softly, again. 'I want to get hold of it. Stand still or it will go away!'

Tom and Dan and Em stood still. They were so happy to have found Ben they did just what he said. They could only just see him. He was lying down in the grass and looking at something. He was holding out his hands. No one spoke. All the time the smoke blew this way and that.

'That's it,' said Ben at last. He held

one hand over the other. He slipped something into the plastic bag and held it tightly so that nothing would get out. He stood up slowly and smiled at the children.

'I was poking the ash. then I saw – well, I couldn't believe my eyes.'

'What is it?'

'We'll get it home first,' said Ben. 'You can't see it here. It's too dark! Besides, it's time for Tom to get his mum's tea. She must be hungry by now. Come on!'

The children walked behind Ben. As he went Ben was silent as if he had something on his mind. He walked slowly and held the plastic bag with great care. When he got to Tom's house he went very slowly up the steps. Tom let them in.

He was happy to be home. He was happy to stand in the hall and to hear Mum call down the stairs.

'Nice to have you back,' she shouted.

'It's nice to be back,' shouted Tom.

'It's nice to be here,' shouted Dan and Em together.

'You must get your mum's tea first,' said Ben to Tom. 'She must need it.'

They all went into the kitchen. The children longed to know what was inside the plastic bag but they knew Ben would not tell them yet. They had to get the tea first. Tom spread sliced bread with butter and jam. Em made the tea and Dan put a plate and cup on to a tray. Ben did nothing. He sat down with the plastic bag in his lap. He was very still.

Tom took the tray up to Mum.

'I've had a lovely sleep,' she said. 'All the afternoon. You never sleep in hospitals, you know. Where have you been?'

'We went back to the bonfire,' said Tom. 'Ben found something. It's in a plastic bag. We don't know what it is! Please, Mum, can we all go up to the attic?'

Mum smiled. 'Of course you can! Aunt Pat isn't here any more.'

Tom smiled as well. He felt free now Mum was back. He felt at home. He ran downstairs.

'We *can* go up to the attic,' he told the others.

'It's good to have your mum back,' said Ben.

They all went upstairs. Dan and Em and Tom sat on the bed while Ben held the bag with care.

Tom smiled. 'Welcome back and welcome to the Time Street Gang,' he said to Ben. 'This time you must say the password with us.'

The twins nodded.

'DEMON MAT DEMON MAT DEMON MAT,' they all said together. Then Ben stood up.

'I need three things. I need a plastic box and some stones and some flies.'

'Flies?' said Em.

'There's no flies here,' said Tom, 'not since Aunt Pat put down the bleach.'

'Never mind,' said Ben. 'I have some in the pet shop. I might even have some in my pocket.'

'There's lots of stones in the back garden,' said Tom.

He ran downstairs and came back with some stones and a plastic box.

'I found the box in the garden. Aunt Pat put all Mum's plastic boxes in the garden. She was going to give them to the dustman. She said they were too old to keep.'

The box had a tight lid.

'We must make tiny holes in it,' said Ben. He had a screw-driver in his pocket and he made some holes in the lid. He also had some dead flies in his pocket.

'These will do,' he said.

'Do you always have dead flies in your pocket?' said Tom.

Ben smiled. 'Not always,' he said.

He put the dead flies into the box. Then he shook the plastic bag into the box. He pulled back the bag and pushed down the lid.

There was something inside the box!

'It's real,' said Ben.

Tom could not believe his eyes. Nor could Em. Nor could Dan. Em put her hand to her mouth as if she was going to scream. Dan looked hard at the plastic box. He was so surprised he could not speak! As for Tom, he could only think of Dad. He would have to tell Dad!

13

Guy

Inside the box was a very small dinosaur. He was grey-brown with feet that looked like hands.

'It must have been the heat from the bonfire,' said Ben.

'What do you mean?' said Tom.

'Well, it must have been the heat from the bonfire that hatched the dinosaur egg. That's why we couldn't find the egg! It had already hatched.'

'I can't believe my eyes,' said Tom.

'Tomorrow after work I'll bring you a bigger box for him,' said Ben, 'but he'll be all right tonight.'

'What shall we call him?' said Em.

They all thought.

'I know,' said Dan, 'let's call him Guy. After Guy Fawkes.'

'Guy,' said Tom. 'It seems to suit him, Hallo, Guy.'

'You must make up a poem,' said Em to Ben. 'Like you always do. We need a poem.'

Ben thought for a moment.

'Guy is a little dinosaur
The smallest one you ever saw!
He must be something of a wizard
To hatch out like a common lizard.'

'That's great,' said Em.

Ben smiled. 'It's my dad in me.'

'My dad would like it,' said Tom. 'I'm going to write to him about Guy.'

'He'll like that,' said Ben. 'But first you must put Guy in the attic with Dr Who. He'll be safe and happy for the winter. But in the spring you might have to let him go. It's only fair.'

Tom frowned. 'Why's that?'

'Dinosaurs like to be free,' said Ben. 'He'll like the heath.'

Tom remembered how shut in he had felt with Aunt Pat. Ben was right. It was good to feel free.

'It's ages until the spring,' said Em. 'We'll be $10^1/_2$ then.'

Dan took out a pencil. 'We can keep notes about Guy. How much he grows.

How much he eats.'

Ben put the plastic box into the attic. 'A good idea! But I don't know if Guy *will* grow. He had such a funny birth. He might stay small.'

'I don't mind if he stays small,' said Tom as they all crept into the attic to see what Dr Who thought of Guy.

The next day went very slowly at school. Tom and Dan and Em could not wait to get back to see if Guy had grown.

After school they ran up to the attic. Guy had eaten all his flies but he was no bigger.

After work Ben brought round a box. It had a light in its lid that ran off a battery. He put a few stones on the floor of the box.

'This will keep Guy happy,' he said. 'The light will warm the stones. Dinosaurs like warm stones.'

'Perhaps he'll begin to grow now,' said Em.

But the next day Guy was just the same. And the next and the next.

One day Dan came in with a book. 'I have been reading that not all dinosaurs were big. And Guy might be adapting himself to the box.'

Tom frowned. 'What do you mean?'

'He might stay small in the box because he can't grow too big in it. When he's free on the heath he might get big.'

'We can't let him out until the spring,' said Tom firmly.

All that winter Guy lived in the attic with Dr Who. The mouse was always bigger than Guy. He often looked at the little dinosaur.

'It's the light he likes,' said Tom.

The smell of bleach had long since gone. Now there was a wonderful smell of mouse and dinosaur. Mum said she liked the smell. She said she would never ask Aunt Pat round while the animals were in the attic.

Mum could see a little better and she often came up to the attic to watch Guy.

'He must be the smallest dinosaur in the world,' she said.

'You wait until the spring,' said Tom.

Dan kept up his notes. He put down what Guy ate each day and what he looked like. He kept the notebook in the attic beside the dinosaur's box.

At last it was spring. Flowers grew on the

heath. The sky above Time Street was blue.

'The time has come to let Guy go,' said Ben.

That night Tom put his duvet down on the attic floor. He lay very close to Guy. He talked to his dinosaur for a long time. Then he wrote a note to Dad.

'I'm letting Guy go,' he wrote. 'It isn't fair if he's always in a box. I wish you had come back to see him. He's still very small but he might grow when he's on the heath. He'll be free on the heath. He needs to be free like us.'

Tom had a lot more to say, but he was very tired. He put down his pencil and paper, then he put out his torch.

It was time to go to sleep.